THE MOST INFLUENTIAL

FEMALE

ACTIVISTS

THE MOST INFLUENTIAL
FEMALE
ACTIVISTS

ERIN STALEY

Rosen
YA
New York

Published in 2019 by The Rosen Publishing Group, Inc.
29 East 21st Street, New York, NY 10010

Library of Congress Cataloging-in-Publication Data

Names: Staley, Erin, author.
Title: The most influential female activists / Erin Staley.
Description: New York : Rosen Publishing, 2019 | Series: Breaking the glass ceiling: The most influential women | Audience: Grades 7–12. | Includes bibliographical references and index.
Identifiers: LCCN 2017049217| ISBN 9781508179634 (library bound) | ISBN 9781508179788 (pbk.)
Subjects: LCSH: Women civil rights workers—Biography—Juvenile literature.
Classification: LCC JC571 .S774 2018 | DDC 323.092/52—dc23
LC record available at https://lccn.loc.gov/2017049217

Manufactured in the United States of America

On the cover: Malala Yousafzai is admired the world over for her work advocating for access to education.

CONTENTS

The citizens of the world deserve to thrive, to be free, and to lead healthy lives without fear, discrimination, and violence. But when injustices exist, activists stand up and speak out.

Activists come in all shapes and sizes. They speak various languages and have different cultures and beliefs. Each has a story to share, a plan to achieve, and a community to elevate. They are doctors, lawyers, government officials, celebrities, pageant queens, and students. For some, activism found them. For others, it is their reason for existence. Their advocacy touches causes such as human rights, gender and sexuality, health and wellness, education, the environment, and the workplace.

Many causes overlap because issues inherently involve each other. Still, specialties are common. Some activists lead national and international nonprofit organizations or conscientious businesses. Others start grassroots endeavors, a term describing a start-up effort or organization. And then there are the allies, those who are as much a part of the effort as the organizers. They offer encouragement, networking opportunities, funding, resources, and, perhaps most important, helping hands.

Activists identify with different genders, but of interest in this treatment are women.

Women take to the streets in New York City in 1915 to advocate for their right to vote and hold elected office.

Regardless of the subject, it is important to note that any historical accounts come from storytellers. These storytellers have their own biases and may omit relevant facts. And some stories are forever lost. In many cases, influential female activists have not always had control of telling their stories.

While it may seem that so much change and attitude shifting have been done thus far, there is still much more to achieve. Great strides are still needed in regards to immigration, access to health care, freedom of expression, and equal pay for equal work. The list goes on and on.

It is likely that more global citizens will come forward to engage in social change. They will share their knowledge, talents, and resources, and they will tackle the tough problems of their times. They will come up with ideas that inspire and compel society to take action. And they will need allies to support them, to give them hope, to celebrate their achievements, and to share their stories to the best of their abilities with the next generation.

CHAPTER ONE

THE FIGHT AGAINST SECOND-CLASS CITIZENSHIP

Often activism begins when freedoms are denied to keep people from having the right to control themselves. Slavery, as a global, imperial enterprise, faced resistance from both slaves and black and white abolitionists. The end of the American Civil War birthed a new form of discrimination against black people. Aboriginal peoples also faced discrimination that made them into a lower class of citizen, if they were granted citizenship at all. Religion was also a factor that oppressors pointed to as justification for discrimination.

Escaping Slavery on the Underground Railroad

In 1777, Vermont became the first (future) state to abolish slavery. Other Northern states followed. Southern states were not interested in ending slavery because their economy depended on it. The life of Harriet Tubman is a testament to how slaves felt about being slaves.

Harriet Tubman was born into slavery in Maryland circa 1820. She used the Underground Railroad to escape to Pennsylvania in 1849. The Underground Railroad was a network of safe houses that temporarily sheltered escapees. Conductors helped passengers travel between safe houses along the network. It was dangerous work that slaveholders were violently hostile toward.

Meanwhile, political battles erupted between abolitionists and slave owners, and compromises were made to prevent civil war. One such compromise allowed California to join the Union as a free state in exchange for passage of the Fugitive Slave Act of 1850, which gave more power to slave owners in Southern states. The Fugitive Slave Act of 1793 made it legal for Southern slaves who escaped to Northern states to be returned to their owners, but in *Prigg v. Pennsylvania*, the Supreme Court ruled that states didn't have to help in that effort. With the Fugitive Slave Act of 1850, Northerners now faced harsh penalties if they did not help capture and return runaway slaves. Slaves and Northern abolitionists alike resented that a federal law would make them complicit in reinforcing the slave status of runaways.

After Tubman's escape, she became one of the most well-known conductors of the Underground Railroad. Tubman became a conductor and risked her life to help slaves escape to Canada.

The Civil Rights Movement

After the Civil War, the Thirteenth Amendment abolished slavery, except in the case of imprisonment. However, the resolution of the war included no remedy for hostility toward black people. Discrimination thus still existed, especially in the South. Jim Crow segregation laws made sure of that.

Just as conductors of the Underground Railroad worked against slavery, activists in the civil rights movement (1954–1968) worked against discrimination in an organized and well-coordinated campaign. Some key women made important breakthroughs in the civil rights movement.

Rosa Parks is known for her part in refusing to give up her seat to a white passenger on a bus in Montgomery, Alabama. The plan was for her to get arrested and for the black community to begin boycotting the local bus system in protest of segregation. As planned, she was arrested, and the black community reacted with a massive boycott of

Ella Josephine Baker was known for teaming up with emerging leaders in her efforts to achieve civil rights for African Americans.

the local bus system on December 5, 1955. After
a little over a year, bus segregation ended when
Browder v. Gayle, a Supreme Court case that declared
Montgomery's segregation laws unconstitutional, went
into effect.

Ella Josephine Baker (1903–1986) was another
key figure during the movement. She grew up listening
to her grandmother's stories of slavery. They inspired
her to seek social justice. After college, she moved
to New York City to support economic justice for the
black community.

Baker believed that no one could be free unless
he or she had a job. In 1940, she joined the National
Association for the Advancement of Colored People
(NAACP). She cofounded a group called In Friendship
to raise the much-needed funds to fight Jim Crow laws,
and she helped Dr. Martin Luther King Jr. organize the
Southern Christian Leadership Conference (SCLC).
Baker also headed the Crusade for Citizenship to
promote voter registration among blacks.

When black college students held a sit-in to protest
being denied service at a Woolworth's lunch counter
in North Carolina, Baker realized how influential youth
could be. She set up a meeting of sit-in leaders, and
this led to the creation of the Student Nonviolent
Coordinating Committee (SNCC). SNCC supported civil
rights activism on college campuses.

Baker's work also helped to ratify the Civil Rights
Act and the Voting Rights Act for African Americans in
the mid-1960s.

Opal Tometi, Patrisse Cullors, and Alicia Garza (*left to right*) are honored during the 2016 Glamour Women of the Year Awards.

Continuing the Fight

Despite the Civil Rights Act of 1964, the civil rights movement never completely achieved its goals of economic and social equality. In 2012, George Zimmerman fatally shot an unarmed seventeen-year-old named Trayvon Martin in Sanford, Florida. Although Zimmerman clearly stalked and killed Martin, Zimmerman claimed self-defense and was acquitted of murder.

These events enraged the black community and its allies. Alicia Garza, Patrisse Cullors, and Opal Tometi created a movement called Black Lives Matter in reaction to the injustice of Martin's killing. The phrase "black lives matter" is an affirmation of the value of black life. It calls attention to the need for American society to treat the black community as equals, something it hasn't done for centuries. But critics tend to assume that the meaning of the phrase is that *only* black lives matter or that black lives matter more—this refusal to attempt to understand takes attention away from the country's long history of racial oppression and the dangers of the racial inequality that still exists for black people in the United States today.

Black Lives Matter activists work toward policing reforms, ending the school-to-prison pipeline, increasing economic opportunity for those who have been let out of prison, and ending racial injustice. One of their means of achieving their goals is reaching out to political professionals such as congresspeople in order to influence political platforms to take into account the needs of people of color and the poor. They also reach out to the community to mobilize, and they organize protests. Their ultimate goal is for people of color to have the same opportunity as their white counterparts.

Fighting for the Rights of Indigenous Peoples

Indigenous peoples are those who have a historical relationship with a place. Their ancestors, members of early civilizations, were the first to migrate to their land. They exist on almost every continent and have historically been forced to adopt the colonizing society's language, culture, and religion.

Many indigenous peoples suffer from discrimination, abuse, imprisonment, or genocide of a cultural or corporeal nature. Some activists stand up for the rights and heritage of indigenous peoples. One such activist is internationally renowned singer/songwriter Buffy Sainte-Marie. Sainte-Marie was born in 1941 on a Cree reserve in Saskatchewan, Canada. After her parents died, relatives in Massachusetts adopted her. She studied education and Oriental philosophy in college and became a successful performing artist with antiwar and human rights songs. In 1969, she funded the Nihewan Foundation for Native American Education. She tells Vogue.com's Alex Frank:

> I really set out to address the problem I saw in Indian country where Indian kids would graduate from high school, want to go to college, but didn't know how to negotiate the path to college. They didn't know how to get a scholarship, they weren't connected by family and friends. I have an Academy Award, but that's not my biggest honor. My biggest honor was to find out that two of my early scholarship recipients had gone on to found tribal colleges. Can you imagine that kind of thrill?

THE NOBEL PEACE PRIZE

The Nobel Peace Prize is an annual award given to those who make outstanding contributions to mankind. It is named after Swedish scientist Alfred Nobel. He invented dynamite, which made him very wealthy. However, Nobel's connections with Austrian-Bohemian pacifist Bertha von Suttner fostered an interest in peace and social issues.

When Nobel died, he left instructions in his will: his money should go toward annual prizes in chemistry, economics, literature, medicine, peace, and physics. Recipients, known as laureates, receive a gold medal, diploma, and a cash prize. The first prizes were given in 1901, and more than one hundred prizes have been distributed since. The first female to receive the honor was Marie Curie, who shared the Nobel Prize for Physics for the research she did on radiation in 1903. Other female Nobel laureates include Mother Teresa, Wangari Maathai, and Malala Yousafzai—each of them was awarded the Nobel Peace Prize.

Rigoberta Menchú, born in Guatemala in 1959, was raised in a low-income family in the Quiche branch of the Mayan culture. Oppression was common, and as a teen, she participated in social reform and women's rights activities.

When a plantation owner was killed, her family was accused of being a part of a local guerrilla organization. Her father was jailed and tortured. Following his release, he joined the Peasant Unity Committee (CUC), a national organization formed by Guatemalan indigenous peoples in defense of their land, food, and water. The CUC defied mining, dam, and industrial agriculture corporations that were guilty of land grabbing, environmental damage, and displacement. The organization advocates for indigenous peasant peoples' rights and ethno-cultural reconciliation. Menchú joined too.

Within a few years, her father, mother, and brother were arrested and murdered. Menchú's commitment deepened. She learned Spanish and several Mayan languages to help during demonstrations. She even helped indigenous people resist massive military oppression. She fled death threats and went to Mexico to continue resistance efforts. For her lifelong activism, Menchú became the first indigenous woman to receive the Nobel Peace Prize.

Campaigning for Water and Food

There are other forms of neglect or harm that government institutions inflict on people. Basic needs aren't met for many people: 795 million people suffer from hunger, and 783 million cannot access clean water. United Nations (UN) delegate and Tanzanian national Anna Tibaijuka (1950–) works to put food on international tables. As executive

Eight-year-old Amariyanna "Mari" Copeny gives President Barack Obama a hug during his May 4, 2016, visit to Flint, Michigan.

director of the United Nations Human Settlements Programme (UN-HABITAT), her mission is to improve the quality of life for 100 million hungry people by 2020. Tibaijuka encourages international lawmakers to help, regardless of financial crises and climate changes that drive food and energy costs up. She also explains that women make great sacrifices to feed their families. They skip meals, decline medical treatment, and prostitute themselves for food. Tibaijuka's activism has led to long-term, effective research and programming.

In Flint, Michigan, lead-filled water that wasn't fit for human consumption reached emergency status following a 2014 change in the city's water supply. Improperly treated water and old pipes prevented community members from drinking from the tap and taking baths. In 2016, Amariyanna "Mari" Copeny (known as Little Miss Flint) wrote a letter to President Barack Obama. The eight-year-old told him she'd been protesting to help other children. Obama responded, saying he'd come to Flint to help. By 2017, the Environmental Protection Agency used $100 million to upgrade Flint's water infrastructure, thanks to funds approved by the Obama administration.

Starting a Conversation

Protests are illegal in Saudi Arabia, and journalists have a hard time getting stories out of the country. But this did not deter Safa al-Ahmad, the creator of a documentary called *Saudi's Secret Uprising* (2014). She used hidden cameras to film the Shia, a religious minority and followers of a sect of Islam, as they raised their voices against poverty and discrimination from a Sunni majority in her home country of Saudi Arabia. While both Islamic sects share similar religious beliefs, their differences have put them at odds for generations. The peaceful protests of the Shia Muslims turned deadly when the police attacked and arrested the nonviolent Shia activists they encountered.

During a Washington parade, Sophie Cruz delivers a letter to Pope Francis. It was an expression of concern for her parents, and others, who are in the United States illegally.

Al-Ahmad's film started a conversation within Saudi Arabia to give equality to everyone living within its borders.

Sophie and the Pope

There are eleven million undocumented immigrants in the United States. Some say they put a strain on resources. Others argue that the United States is a nation of immigrants. To date, more than two million immigrants have been deported, leaving behind thousands of children. Activists speak volumes about this topic—one in particular. When Pope Francis visited Washington, DC, in 2015, five-year-old Sophie Cruz broke through a barricade to hand him a letter. In it, she asked him to prevent the deportation of her parents, who had illegally migrated from Mexico. Today, she is one of the many youths affected by Deferred Action for Childhood Arrivals (DACA), which protects qualifying immigrant youth from being deported. In 2017, Sophie won the Define American Award for Activist of the Year and addressed thousands at the Women's March on Washington.

ANSWERING THE CALL FOR WOMEN AND CHILDREN

Historically, women and children have been treated as second-class citizens. Self-awareness led many women to advocate for what they were denied by their homeland. These were struggles that, in time, have found a great deal of success overall.

"Ain't I a Woman?"

Sojourner Truth, born around 1797, was an abolitionist from New York. Her activism included suffrage, prison reform, and anti–capital punishment advocacy. She escaped slavery and won a court battle to get her son back after he was illegally sold.

Sojourner Truth is respected for sharing her voice, writing her memoirs, and taking a stand in the fight for human rights.

Truth toured the country to tell her story and promote human rights. In 1851, she attended the Women's Rights Convention in Akron, Ohio. Women were declared to be weak and intellectually inferior, and they were denied equal rights to men. Truth took to her feet and debunked the idea that women require special treatment because they were thought to be weak in her speech "Ain't I a Woman?" It was charged with her experiences as a female slave and how tough she had to be to endure. Truth had been sold several times (the first time at the age of nine), denied a relationship with the man who fathered her first child, and forced into marriage. She spoke of the lack of consideration she'd received and pointed out that every woman, regardless of color, ought to be treated with respect and equality.

The Right to Vote

The United States passed the Nineteenth Amendment to the US Constitution in 1920. It took seventy-two years for the women's rights movement in the United States to prevail.

The movement began with the Seneca Falls Convention. Lucretia Mott and Elizabeth Cady Stanton held the event in Seneca Falls, New York, in 1848. The convention produced the Declaration of Sentiments, a proclamation with language that was similar to the nation's Declaration of Independence. It declared that women and men are equal and should all be able to vote and pursue happiness in their lives.

Action was needed next. Two national women's suffrage associations were created, and protests were held in the nation's capital. Arrests were made, and hunger strikes influenced lawmakers. In 1920, the Nineteenth Amendment was ratified. Other nations followed over the years, with Saudi Arabia in 2011.

American Feminism

Feminism is a movement that advocates ending inequalities and discriminations against women in male-dominated societies. It takes into account the roles and relationships of women on all levels, from social to sexual and economics to politics. Feminism gained momentum in the nineteenth century with the Seneca Falls Convention and again in the 1960s as more modern feminists emerged, including Gloria Steinem.

Steinem studied government and the modern interests of women while attending Smith College in Massachusetts. After graduation, she became a freelance writer. For one of her most famous pieces, she went undercover in New York City's Playboy Club to expose gender inequality.

In the late 1960s, Steinem helped create *New York* magazine. Her writing in the magazine touched on politics and important issues in the women's movement. In 1971, she helped to create the National Women's Political Caucus, a multiparty organization that supports females seeking political office. In the early 1970s, she cocreated *Ms.* magazine, a liberal feminist publication.

During her long career, she has realized that endurance is what's needed to see things change. Steinem explains in a 1992 People.com article, "We need to be long-distance runners to make a real social revolution. And you can't be a long-distance runner unless you have some inner strength."

The Emergence of Brazilian Feminism

Feminism blossomed in Brazil in the mid-1970s. Organizations focused on female sexuality, health, education, and domestic violence. Inspired, Míriam Martinho started the nation's first lesbian feminist organization, Grupo Lésbico-Feminista, in 1979. It split after two years.

Some members, including Martinho, formed Grupo Ação

Gloria Steinem, a feminist icon, is known for her celebration of women, their accomplishments, and the benefits of gender equality.

Lésbica-Feminista (GALF). In 1981, GALF began publishing *ChanacomChana*, Brazil's first activist newspaper. It called for the inclusion of lesbians in the feminist movement and became the catalyst behind "Brazil's Stonewall." The first Stonewall was a violent protest by the LGBTQ+ community after police raided the Stonewall Inn in New York City in 1969.

CELEBRATING INTERNATIONAL WOMEN'S DAY

International Women's Day (IWD) honors the cultural, economic, political, and social accomplishments of women. Events include craft markets, political rallies, performances, and business conferences.

The idea for an annual celebration has roots in a 1908 march in New York City. About fifteen thousand women took to the streets calling for voting rights, shorter work hours, and better pay.

In 1909, the United States observed its first National Women's Day. In 1910, Social Democratic Party member Clara Zetkin, a German, proposed honoring an annual women's day on the same date each year. The first IWD was celebrated in Austria, Denmark, Germany, and Switzerland on March 19, 1911. Two years later, March 8 became the official IWD. The UN celebrated IWD for the first time in 1975.

The events leading up to Brazil's Stonewall occurred at Ferro's Bar in São Paulo in 1983. The bar had a lesbian clientele, but the owners kicked Martinho and a colleague out when they tried to distribute *ChanacomChana*. A physical altercation ensued, and the paper was banned from the bar.

Martinho called for a nonviolent demonstration. Afterwards, Ferro's Bar developed an even larger lesbian clientele! In 1989, GALF became the nonprofit organization (NPO) called Um Outro Olhar. The paper assumed the same name and continued to report on feminist issues such as health care for lesbians.

A Voice for the Voiceless

Women and girls are our most vulnerable population. Often without resources and recourse, they depend on activists like Sampat Pal Devi for help. She is from Banda District in Uttar Pradesh, a state in India. The district has a rigid caste system and is highly patriarchal. Women are powerless to the effects of illiteracy and financial dependence and often fall prey to physical and sexual abuse and child marriages.

To deal with these issues, Sampat Pal Devi created a vigilante movement called the Gulabi Gang. It is made up of more than one hundred thousand women who defend themselves against oppressive fathers, husbands, brothers, and corrupt government officials. Gang members march in pink saris and confront offenders. They confront in a nonviolent manner, but if the offender doesn't reform, the women defend their cause with wooden staffs. The Gulabi Gang also built a school to teach children skills to earn money for their families.

Another force for women's and girls' rights is Malalai Joya. She grew up in refugee camps in Iran and Pakistan. Her home country of Afghanistan had been torn apart by war, foreign occupation, warlords, and corrupt government officials. Millions fled to neighboring countries as the Taliban rose to power and enforced extreme Islamist fundamentalism.

Brave women and their male allies often join Gulabi Gang leader Sampat Pal Devi (*front row, right*) in protest of violence against woman.

The Taliban's restrictions were grave, especially for women. Females were forced to wear head-to-toe burqas and walk with chaperones. Girls became child brides and were forbidden from going to school.

At twenty-five, Joya stood up at a constitutional assembly and denounced the ongoing violations of women's rights. Two years later, she was elected to Afghanistan's new Parliament—its youngest member. Her criticisms continued, and Joya was banished. Multiple assassination attempts were made on her life, and now she only travels with bodyguards and

Despite being removed as a member of the Afghan parliament, Malalai Joya has received international acclaim for speaking out for human and women's rights.

sleeps in safe houses. In fact, the name "Joya" is a moniker that she uses to preserve her safety and the safety of her family. She wrote in her book *A Woman Among Warlords: The Extraordinary Story of an Afghan Who Dared to Raise Her Voice*, "I am not afraid of an early death if it would advance the cause of justice. Even the grave cannot silence my voice, because there are others who would carry on after me."

MATTERS OF GENDER AND SEXUAL AUTONOMY

All women should be able to freely express their gender and sexuality. Yet, societies have often dictated that they cannot. Often, this control goes beyond control over women. Children and sexual and gender minorities were also placed in a subjugated position.

Going Viral with Hooligan Sparrow

Human trafficking is a multibillion dollar industry. It exists in more than one hundred countries and includes sex and domestic labor. Traffickers use

Ye Haiyan, a Chinese activist, has been forced to move from city to city to avoid harassment for her efforts to prevent human sex trafficking.

coercion, such as violence, blackmail, and debt bondage, to force men, women, and children into slavery. Activists like Ye Haiyan, a Chinese woman known as Hooligan Sparrow, work tirelessly to prevent human trafficking and to change the law to protect targets.

Ye, who draws a huge following on Chinese social media, is partially known for her advocacy for women who are either sex workers or have been sexually abused. After becoming known for this work, she learned of the story of six female students between the ages of eleven and fourteen. A school principal and a government official took the girls to an out-of-town hotel.

In China, the age of sexual consent is fourteen. If the child is under fourteen, sexual activity is considered child rape. The crime is punishable by life in prison or death. If the guilty party is involved in child sex trafficking, the crime is punishable with a jail sentence of five to fifteen years.

However, in the case of the six girls, it was revealed that the principal and government official paid $2,000 to the girls to have sex with them. Because of a now-repealed law, it would have meant the girls would be charged with prostitution, and the rapists would go free.

Ye and her allies opposed this law with a protest. They held signs with messages like "Get a room with me; leave the kids alone." Ye's protest cast a negative light on the government, and she and her allies became enemies of the state. They were harassed and interrogated for their action.

Filmmaker Nanfu Wang captured the story in her documentary *Hooligan Sparrow*. People from all over the world shared similar situations, giving Wang hope that her film and Ye's efforts have started the conversation for change.

Defying the Threats to Expose the Truth

Being an activist was a life-threatening career for Mexican journalist Lydia Cacho. A tip came to Cacho that a man was using girls between the ages of four and thirteen to create explicit pornographic materials. Cacho investigated and learned the human trafficking network had international ties.

In 2003, she blew the lid off of a human trafficking ring in Cancun. She wrote a book about the investigation and quickly began to receive death threats. Police officers then kidnapped her at gunpoint in 2005. Cacho was taken out of town and tortured.

A call from an unidentified person resulted in her safe return. Cacho continues to write and address international audiences about detecting and preventing global sex trafficking, and about healing for those who have experienced child sexual abuse. But she fled Mexico to preserve her safety.

Mexican activist Lydia Cacho has been threatened, tortured, and thrown in jail for demanding justice be done to those who practice human trafficking.

She believes the only way she can return is if she exposes the person who tried to have her killed.

Despite the attempts at silencing her, her work didn't go unnoticed. She received the Civil Courage Prize and was named a World Press Freedom Hero by the International Press Institute.

ON THE LOOKOUT FOR HUMAN TRAFFICKING

Human trafficking can happen to anyone—nationals, foreigners, abled and disabled persons, men, women, children, and those from the LGBTQ+ community. It's important to know the signs in order to help others.

Some signs are malnourishment, poor health, and signs of restraint or torture. Victims may not be free to come and go, they may be denied work breaks, they may live or work in highly restrictive areas, or they may work long hours. Victims may divert eye contact or tense up when law enforcement officers come near them. They may be anxious, depressed, disoriented, afraid, paranoid, or submissive. They may bring home huge amounts of money or have staggering debts.

If you think something's off, reach out to an adult. Or, contact the National Human Trafficking Hotline at (888) 373-7888, humantraffickinghotline.org, or text HELP to BeFree (233733). In Canada, contact Chrysalis Anti-Human Trafficking Network at (866) 528-7109 or at chrysalisnetwork.org.

A Thorn in the Paw of Sexual Exploitation

Sexual trafficking and child sexual exploitation are not limited to in-person contact. They are also found on the dark web. Youths connect to perpetrators online and are made to feel important. When they meet, the unsuspecting youths fall victim to abuse, rape, and are often sold or trapped into human trafficking rings. Compelled to do something about this, celebrities Demi Moore and Ashton Kutcher cofounded what's now known as Thorn: Digital Defenders of Children. It raises funds to build antitrafficking software. Within six months, one of Thorn's projects uncovered more than six thousand incidents of trafficking, two thousand of which involved minors. It also reduced investigation time by 60 percent.

Bagels to Sustain Support and Self-Confidence

When civil war broke out in Serbia in 1991, it created a humanitarian crisis that sent millions of people fleeing to neighboring countries. Many were forced to live in temporary housing, and many women and children fell victim to violence and human trafficking.

In response, Marijana Savic created Atina in 2004 to address the issue. She is an antiwar, antimisogyny, and pro–LGBTQ+ rights activist. Atina is a nonprofit organization that offers basic needs, education, and help with legal, medical, and psychosocial needs to refugees. Funding came from governments and international donations, but Savic realized the assistance was tough to sustain. Atina needed a steady source of funding.

Atina created a bagel business in Belgrade. Eight months and five hundred recipes later, they had the perfect bagel. The company was named Bagel Бејгл (Bagel Bejgl). It offered steady funding for housing and support services. It also gave survivors financial independence, a boost in self-worth, and a way to contribute to the community. One of their most famous customers was Camilla, Duchess of Cornwall, who visited during her 2016 stay in Belgrade.

Lesbian Pride

The LGBTQ+ community and their allies work to have their rights be acknowledged and protected by the law.

Audre Lorde called herself a "black, lesbian, feminist, mother, warrior, poet." She was born in 1934 in Harlem to West Indian parents. Despite poor eyesight, she became an avid reader. Poetry was her passion, and she was first published as a teenager.

Lorde's first collection of poems was *The First Cities* (1968). In it, she voiced her disdain for ageism,

Audre Lorde earned her master's degree from Columbia University, worked as a librarian, and became an active member of the LGBTQ+ community.

classism, homophobia, racism, and sexism. Lorde received numerous awards, including a grant from the National Endowment for the Arts. When asked what writers can learn from her, Lorde says in her book *Conversations with Audre Lorde*, "I can tell them not to be afraid to feel and not to be afraid to write about it. Even if you are afraid, do it anyway. We learn to work when we are tired, so we can learn to work when we are afraid."

The Enduring Difficulties of Lesbians

Former Czechoslovakian, and now American, tennis champion Martina Navratilova (born 1956) is one of the world's first professional athletes to come out publicly. She announced her sexual orientation in 1981. The news cost her millions in sponsorships and endorsement deals. But Navratilova wasn't willing to pretend to be something she wasn't. She was going to freely live as she was: a lesbian woman.

Similarly, South African Funeka Soldaat considers herself to be an "out and proud" lesbian and activist. She survived corrective rape, a hate crime performed because of one's perceived sexuality or gender identity. She sought help from the police, but they only assaulted her and threw her into a squad car and into a jail cell. The incident fueled Soldaat's resolve to help those who weren't safe. In

2008, Soldaat cofounded Free Gender, a nonprofit organization that demands justice for LGBTQ+ community members who suffer hate crimes.

Transgender Women's Stories

Laverne Cox is not only an award-winning actress but also an activist for transgender issues. She speaks candidly about her experiences as a transgender woman and about the courage it took to be on the outside what she is on the inside. Cox identifies the struggles the transgender community faces, including self-acceptance, mental-health issues, and discrimination.

Cox often takes her advocacy on tour by speaking to college students in the United States and Canada. Her speech "Ain't I a Woman: My Journey to Womanhood" borrows from Sojourner Truth's speech. Cox calls for equality across genders and ethnicities and encourages others to look beyond gender assignment.

When Dr. Lydia Foy was born in Ireland in 1947, she was assigned a male identity. She became a target for bullying in school and watched as two other transgender classmates suffered—one of whom committed suicide.

Foy suffered from a nervous breakdown as an adult. Foy lived life as a male and married and had two children.

Dr. Lydia Foy took on the Irish government in an effort to be officially recognized as female on her legal documents.

Two years before her gender reassignment surgery, she began to present herself as female. Again, Dr. Foy was subjected to discrimination. One year after the surgery, she applied for a new birth certificate that reflected her gender identity. The request was denied. A legal battle ensued for several decades, and Foy advocated publicly for the right for full legal recognition of gender with new birth certificates. In 2015, the Gender Recognition Act was passed in Ireland. It allowed transgender people's preferred gender to be legally recognized. This meant they could be reissued a birth certificate that reflects their gender identity, as well as other benefits.

CHAPTER FOUR

CHANGING THE COURSE OF HEALTH

At one time, women were not thought to be intellectually capable of working in health and medicine. Yet, strong, committed women persevered. They found ways to enter male-dominated medical schools, earn medical degrees, promote prevention, make breakthroughs, and advocate for women. But it wasn't always medical professionals who brought change to their communities.

America's First Woman to Graduate from Medical School

British-American Elizabeth Blackwell (1821–1910) was a pioneer for female doctors but, at one point in her life, hated anything associated with medicine and the human body. When a sick friend described the hardships of being treated by a male physician,

Elizabeth Blackwell, the first female doctor in the United States, was convinced that healthy people lived happier lives and thus a stronger community could be enjoyed by all.

Blackwell's mind was made up. She earned $3,000 for medical school but was denied because of her gender.

A male doctor gave her lessons. She observed him treating patients and lecturing. The Geneva Medical College in New York eventually admitted Blackwell, and she graduated at the top of her class. However, the medical community banned her from practicing medicine.

She went to France to be a midwife, and a resident physician mentored her in obstetrics. When Blackwell returned to the United States, male doctors still refused to work with her. Since she couldn't find a hospital to work for, Blackwell started her own, the New York Infirmary for Women and Children (now the Beekman Downtown Hospital), in 1853. It treated the poor, and it gave female medical students a place to work and train.

Throughout her life, Blackwell made great strides for women in medicine. She wrote about education, sex, and medical sociology, and she started medical schools and national health societies. By her death in 1910, there were more than seven thousand female physicians in the United States.

Contraception Throughout the Ages

Women have historically used various methods of family planning, including birth control and abortion. In ancient Mesopotamia and Egypt, honey and sodium carbonate mixtures and crocodile dung were used as methods of contraception. Ancient Egyptian women also created birth-control devices that were soaked in fermented plant juice.

In Greece, wine, lead, vinegar, and pomegranate were all used as contraceptives. The silphium plant was so effective in North Africa that it was overharvested to the point of extinction. Bamboo, moss, and seaweed were popular contraceptive methods in China and Japan, while cabbage and elephant dung were used as birth control in Persia. Indian women were partial to honey or ghee, while African women used vegetable seedpods, grass, and crushed roots.

In 1484, however, the Catholic Church declared the prevention of pregnancy to be immoral. Women who used or promoted family planning methods were accused of witchery and were subjected to death. This severely squelched the knowledge and availability of birth control methods for centuries.

Eventually, though, contraception reemerged. American Margaret Sanger, and others like her, opened family planning clinics around the world to help women access reproductive health services and resources. The first of these clinics opened in the United States in 1916.

More recently, Brazilian Carmen Barroso has advocated for the sexual and reproductive health and rights in Latin America and in the Caribbean. While earning her doctorate in social psychology, Barroso learned that women are empowered when they access reproductive education and health care.

THE AMERICAN RED CROSS

Bloodshed was massive during the American Civil War (1861–1865). To add to the hardship, food and medical supplies weren't making it to the front lines. Clara Barton (1821–1912) knew it was time to act. She scooped up her own supplies and took them to the soldiers in need.

Barton was declared an angel on the battlefield for her nursing work during the Civil War, and she continued her aid after the war by helping to locate and identify missing soldiers.

Barton's efforts took their toll, and her doctor ordered her to Europe to rest. There, she learned about the International Committee of the Red Cross. It helped wounded soldiers and gave them protection in a neutral setting. Inspired, Barton returned to the United States and established her own institution, the American Red Cross, in 1881.

Over the years, the American Red Cross has helped those in the armed forces, provided global disaster relief, recruited nurses, taught safety and first aid, and shipped supplies to soldiers overseas. It supplies more than 40 percent of the blood and blood products in the United States.

They're free to focus on academic and professional goals and contribute to the community. Barroso stepped up to become executive director for the International Planned Parenthood Federation/Western Hemisphere Region. She worked to prevent teen pregnancy, ensure the health of pregnant women, and make contraception accessible.

Edna Adan Ismail

Female genital mutilation (FGM) is the forcible cutting away of the clitoris and labia. The practice is done for many reasons, including social and religious beliefs. However, medical professionals, activists, and government bodies insist FGM has no justifiable purpose. It causes horrific pain, bleeding, infection, and difficulty with urination, sex, and childbirth. It can even lead to death. Although FGM is illegal in many countries—including the United States and Canada—it's still performed around the world.

At eight years old, Edna Adan Ismail was subjected to FGM. She remembers a deep sense of injustice, and this later fueled her activism. Ismail became a midwife in the mid-1900s and pioneered obstetrics and gynecology as director of the Ministry of Health in Somalia in 1976.

One of her missions was to address the physical consequences of FGM. Ismail worked to pass anti-FGM legislation in the 1970s and 1980s. She also worked with the UN and the World Health Organization (WHO) to educate government leaders, and she included men and religious leaders in the conversation.

While great strides were made, she realized that legislation without enforcement does nothing because the practice is enforced underground.

Edna Adan Ismail credits her strong advocacy to sharing the mission with a team and understanding that to achieve anything takes patience and persistence.

Only ongoing education convinces people that the practice is unacceptable.

When Ismail retired from the United Nations, she used her pension to build the Edna Adan University Hospital in 2001. It serves women in Somaliland, an autonomous region in Somalia, and in surrounding areas.

Jaha Dukureh

Jaha Dukureh, born in the Gambia in 1989 or 1990, also raises awareness about FGM. She started a Change.org campaign to petition President Obama's administration to investigate the impacts of FGM and those Americans who are considered at risk. On the website, Dukureh writes of her experience of being subjected to FGM: "It took away a part of my femininity, my ownership to my body. Some girls, including my half-sister who died from complications from being cut, even lose their lives." Despite being declared a human rights violation by the UN, the practice continues, even in developed countries. She explains, "The practice of FGM is illegal in the US but girls are being taken to other countries, usually their parents' country of origin where they are cut in what is now known as 'vacation cutting.'"

Dukureh's campaign collected more than 221,000 signatures, and these influenced the ban on FGM in the Gambia. The Central African Republic, Egypt, Nigeria, and South Africa also banned FGM. Efforts to end FGM continue in Sierra Leone, where 88 percent of females are cut, and in Somalia, where 98 percent are cut—the highest occurrence in the world.

Changing the Conversation about Mental Health

Although Canadian Clara Hughes won six Summer and Winter Olympic Games medals for speed skating and cycling, she struggled with depression. Hughes first experienced it while training in the

Canadian Clara Hughes takes to the ice to compete in a speed skating event in the 2010 Vancouver Winter Olympics.

mid-1990s. She felt worthless and inadequate. A team doctor diagnosed it as depression, but Hughes didn't want to hear it. She threw herself into training, but she couldn't focus and started crashing her bicycle. Hughes was forced to seek help. She now manages depression successfully.

MODERN HEALTH CARE POLICIES EMERGE

When Franklin D. Roosevelt became US president in 1933, his wife, Eleanor, set out to impact the nation's public health policy. It was during the Great Depression (1929–1939), and families struggled for survival and to afford health care. President Roosevelt initiated programs to help, and First Lady Eleanor Roosevelt traveled by train to see if they were working. She also spoke out against poverty, tackled racism, and fought for legislation to give every citizen their right to health care. Her efforts contributed to the quality of life for all Americans, but she didn't stop with national issues. In 1948, she headed up the UN Human Rights Commission and helped to write the Universal Declaration of Human Rights. It was adopted in 1948 by the United Nations General Assembly and stands as the comprehensive statement of inalienable human rights to which all countries are encouraged to adhere.

When the Olympian learned that a long-time sponsor of hers was hosting a national mental health campaign, she jumped at the chance to be its spokesperson. The company committed $50 million to national mental health initiatives, and Hughes publicly shared her experiences to fight the stigma surrounding poor mental health. To further her advocacy, Hughes completed a 110-day national cycling tour in 2014. She rode for 7,000 miles (11,265 kilometers) around Canada, visited 105 communities, and gave speeches and interviews at more than 235 events to raise awareness and funds for mental health.

Achieving the Dream

About three hundred million females around the world have some form of intellectual, mental, physical, or sensory disability. Many face discrimination, poverty, illiteracy, lack of skills, unemployment, and lower wages than males with similar disabilities. Yetnebersh Nigussie challenged these limitations in Ethiopia after becoming blind at five years old.

Nigussie earned a law degree and a master's in social work. While attending Addis Ababa University, Nigussie founded a female student organization and headed up its anti-AIDS campaign. She was active in twenty volunteer organizations and launched the Ethiopian Center for Disability and Development to

Ethiopian Yetnebersh Nigussie has made great strides in—and has been awarded for—her work to promote the rights of those with disabilities.

include people with disabilities in economic and social programs.

Nigussie was instrumental in establishing new building codes throughout the country that gave greater access to the disabled. She also helped hundreds of women become financially independent. Nigussie told ilo.org, "We should capitalize on people's ability rather than capitalize on their disability and hand them charity. I am a generous person but I don't give people charity." She also expressed that she hopes to lead by example: "I am always looking to see how I can do more, how I can give more. I continue to prove to myself and to my community that I can achieve what I dream."

CHAPTER FIVE

EMPOWERMENT THROUGH EDUCATION

E ducation elevates a community. Creativity abounds, the standard of living increases, and people are happier, healthier, and more empathetic. Yet, many of the world's population are uneducated and unable to access education because of gender discrimination, lack of resources, and social, political, and religious restrictions. Many women have worked to expand access.

Malala Yousafzai

Malala Yousafzai, born in Pakistan in 1997, was just ten years old when the Taliban took control of her community. It began attacking girls' schools, and at age eleven, Malala delivered the speech "How Dare the Taliban Take Away My Basic Right to Education?" She also wrote about her experiences in 2009 on a very public BBC blog.

Women and activists around the world look up to and partner with Pakistani activist Malala Yousafzai to fight for girls' education.

Although Yousafzai used a pen name, her true identity was eventually revealed. For her stance against the Taliban's anti-education policy, she was nominated for the International Children's Peace Prize and won Pakistan's National Youth Peace Prize—both in 2011. The Taliban began to issue death threats against her. While she was riding the bus home from school one day in 2012, a masked gunman came on board and shot her in the head.

No one expected Yousafzai to survive, but after a long recovery, she did. She went on to support other girls fighting for equality and education. In 2013, she co-wrote *I Am Malala: How One Girl Stood Up for Education and Changed the World*. The next year, she won the Nobel Peace Prize, making her the youngest laureate ever. She started the Malala Fund to support the rights of girls. She also encouraged supporters to tell world leaders that education is the greatest weapon. She wrote the following in a 2015 article on malala.org:

> The shocking truth is that world leaders have the money to fully fund primary AND secondary education around the world—but they are choosing to spend it on other things, like their military budgets. In fact, if the whole world stopped spending money on the military for just 8 days, we could have the $39 billion still needed to provide 12 years of free, quality education to every child on the planet.

EDUCATION IN AMERICA

In the 1600s and 1700s in America, a woman's social status and race determined her access to education. If wealthy, she went to school or had a tutor. Lessons included reading, writing, arithmetic, sewing, knitting, and manners. Her gender was limiting. Wealthy males had lessons, too, but they advanced to town schools and universities. If a female were from a middle-class family, she might be permitted to sit in on her brother's lessons.

If she were from a lower class or minority family, lessons were nonexistent. Lower-class male and female children worked alongside their parents for survival.

In the 1800s, white female students began to attend secondary school. Some female educators, such as Catharine Beecher, Mary Lyon, and Emma Willard, opened their own schools. Female students took advanced courses, and academic achievements were equal to those of male students. As the nineteenth century progressed, more women of all ethnicities began to attend college. However, they were not equally represented on campuses until the 1980s.

By the end of the 1900s, federal law required all children, regardless of gender and social class, to attend elementary through secondary school. However, the quality of education varied (and still does) due to wealth, ethnicity, and geographical location.

Ending the Cycle of Poverty with Early Childhood Development

Many people believe that education should begin with early childhood development (ECD). ECD is a topic that is close to the heart of Columbian award-winning singer/songwriter, Shakira. According to Shakira.com:

> *9 million Latin American children younger than 5 years old suffer from chronic malnutrition and 22 million don't have access to education. Malnutrition and the absence of care in the early stages of life are the main mechanisms for the transmission of inequality. This is why experts agree that early childhood development is one of the most effective tools to end with the intergenerational cycle of poverty.*

Shakira is involved in three advocacy projects. Her first, Pies Descalzos Foundation, builds state-of-the-art schools for displaced and underrepresented children. Students get a quality education and nutritious meals, as well as art, music, and recreation enrichment. Their families also learn about local financial opportunities. Shakira's second project is the ALAS Foundation, a nonprofit that encourages the implementation of early childhood public policies in the communities of Latin America. Her third project is working for the UNICEF Goodwill Ambassador program. She establishes political

Shakira served on the President's Advisory Commission on Educational Excellence for Hispanics in the United States and former UK prime minister Gordon Brown's International Commission on Financing Global Education.

initiatives to give children around the world access to education.

Telling the World Their Stories

Congolese Neema Namadamu speaks for disabled persons. At age two, she contracted polio. It left her

TRUE GIRL POWER: INTERNATIONAL DAY OF THE GIRL CHILD

The International Day of the Girl Child is an annual holiday to recognize the rights and challenges of the world's 1.1 billion girls. It was adopted in 2011 by the United Nations General Assembly. UN.org notes:

> If effectively supported during the adolescent years, girls have the potential to change the world—both as the empowered girls of today and as tomorrow's workers, mothers, entrepreneurs, mentors, household heads, and political leaders. An investment in realising the power of adolescent girls upholds their rights today and promises a more equitable and prosperous future, one in which half of humanity is an equal partner in solving the problems of climate change, political conflict, economic growth, disease prevention, and global sustainability.

permanently disabled, but it didn't limit her activism. In high school, she used her weekly radio show to raise awareness. She went on to graduate from college. She became the first woman with a disability to do so in the Congo and the second woman from her tribe to graduate from a national university.

In 2011, Namadamu founded a national telecommunications company, Go Network, to inform and empower women in eastern Congo. She also created the Maman Shujaa Media Center. It gave local women training in digital and internet literacy, and it welcomed them to tell of their challenges and demand peace. Through Word Pulse, an online community reaching more than 190 countries, these stories reach a worldwide audience.

The Power of Inclusion

Poor children aren't the only demographic that has historically been vulnerable to being denied education. Those living with disabilities are another group that has unique challenges. Some have physical issues, some intellectual, and most just want the opportunity to show the world what they can achieve. But achieving requires the help and support of others.

Intellectual disabilities (ID) include autism spectrum disorder, Down syndrome, and cerebral palsy. People with ID may have trouble learning or functioning as quickly and as well as those without ID, which makes them vulnerable to discrimination.

But Eunice Kennedy Shriver, an American, wanted to champion the rights and acceptance of those living with ID. In 1962, she pioneered a summer sports and physical activity camp. It's now known as the Special Olympics. Athletes with ID participate in a wide range of individual and team sports, such as skiing, judo, powerlifting, and badminton. They compete for medals, but the focus is inclusion and community.

Today, the Special Olympics serves more than 4.7 million athletes of all ages from 172 countries. Participation boosts self-confidence, fosters a network of support, and creates global awareness for those living with ID.

Expanding Education to Previously Ignored Groups

Fatima al-Aqel (1957–2012) became an influential figure to the blind in Yemen. Al-Aqel had been raised to value education. She and her sister, both blind, moved to Egypt, where there were more education opportunities. Al-Aqel earned a degree and became a social specialist at Cairo's Al-Noor Institute for Blind Women.

She later returned to Yemen, where her people suffered from high rates of blindness and eye disease. Many could have had restored vision but were too poor to afford the treatments. They

Casar Jacobson attends an observance of International Women's Day in March 2017 at the United Nations in New York City.

also suffered from depression and were financially dependent on others.

To deal with the problems born of blindness and eye disease, al-Aqel established the Yemeni Blind Organization to give women an education and boost their confidence. In 1995, al-Aqel founded a residential school to help them become more socially active. She also founded the Al-Aman Organization for Blind Women Care. The organization printed Braille books and helped students with job placement. In the 2000s, al-Aqel established a kindergarten for blind children and a rehabilitation center for those with cognitive and vision disabilities.

Similarly, Norwegian-Canadian Casar Jacobson was born hard of hearing. She gradually became deaf in her twenties, but it didn't prevent her from winning Miss Canada in 2013. She also won other pageants and, in her run for Miss Globe, was awarded Miss Peace. Jacobson uses these opportunities to speak out for the rights of those with disabilities. She serves as a UN Women Youth Champion and stresses the importance of noninvasive technology to restore hearing. Jacobson also connects those with little or no hearing to entrepreneurial networks and resources to build their own businesses. She notes the following on her website, CasarJacobson.com:

> When we see success, we often don't see disability. When we see disability, we often don't see potential for success. Our mission is to have all countries, cultures and religions get to know the person behind the disability to foster & cultivate education, entrepreneurialism & community involvement.

CHAPTER SIX

BECOMING ONE WITH THE LAND

Our planet is fragile. With limited resources, it is imperative that we work together to reduce our carbon footprint. Many have worked to do this and to put environmental policies in place to care for and protect the land, oceans, and wildlife.

She Multiplied: An Activist's Legacy

Berta Cáceres (ca. 1971–2016) was a member of the indigenous Lenca group living in Honduras. She defended their land rights, which were constantly threatened by organizations that wanted the land for damming and mining projects. Even though laws protected them, the indigenous people didn't have modern-day documents to prove the land was theirs.

Attendees honor Honduran activist Berta Cáceres at her funeral in La Esperanza in 2016. Cáceres is renowned for helping the indigenous Lenca people defend their lands and resources.

In 1993, Cáceres cofounded the National Council of Popular and Indigenous Organizations of Honduras (COPINH). It defended the land rights of more than two hundred Lenca communities. COPINH became very influential, and Cáceres began speaking to international audiences against big industry.

In 2009, Honduras experienced a military coup. The government became more corrupt, and without a strong justice system, it was increasingly dangerous. Targeted populations suffered, including environmental activists. Thousands fled, but Cáceres was unrelenting in her criticism of the government's lack of protection.

In 2010, she thwarted another dam project that would have negatively impacted an area that provided food, water, and a spiritual sanctuary for the Lenca. Threats against her life were issued, and in 2016, she was fatally shot. Others have followed in her footsteps, encouraging themselves with "*Berta no murió, se multiplico,*" meaning "Berta didn't die, she multiplied."

Winona LaDuke is another organizer who fought for land rights. She was born in 1959 in California and is a Jewish Native American from the Ojibwe White Earth Reservation in Minnesota. She is a former US vice presidential candidate and founder of White Earth Land Recovery Project (WELRP). Since 1989, this grassroots organization has been working for the return of land stolen by the United States from the Anishinaabeg people on the White Earth Indian Reservation in Minnesota. WELRP also works to re-instill the harvest of the people's traditional wild rice. LaDuke's efforts with WELRP, as well as her many other environmental justice and sustainable living projects, have been honored throughout the years. In 1998, *Ms.* magazine named her Woman of the Year.

Love Yourself, Love the Environment

Up to one trillion plastic bags are discarded every year around the world. They crowd landfills, taking up to one thousand years to break down. The bags that are collected are sometimes burned in garbage piles, and those burning piles of garbage release harmful dioxins into the air. Many bags clog up drains and rivers and make their way into the oceans. This dispersion is especially dangerous to fish, sea turtles, seabirds, and other wildlife. Many choke after trying to consume the bags, or they are strangled by the straps.

The bags that are labeled "biodegradable" only break down into microplastics. Many governments have encouraged reusable bags by either taxing or banning single-use plastic bags at grocery and liquor stores. These strides in legislation were the result of activists such as Melati and Isabel Wijsen from Bali and Isatou Ceesay from the Gambia.

The Wijsen sisters were adolescents when they took on the overwhelming plastic pollution of Bali.

Less than 5 percent of the island's used plastic bags were recycled. Inspired by activists they discovered in school like Diana, Princess of Wales, and Mahatma Gandhi, the sisters created Bye Bye Plastic Bags in 2013. The goal was to get a petition going to ban plastic bags and to host cleanup events. Youth volunteers joined in, and the organization created an online marketing campaign.

Their efforts paid off. Plastic bags were banned in their village. Next was the governor's office. He signed a promise that Bali would be plastic-free by 2018. The International Airport of Bali encouraged visitors to bring reusable bags. Melati and Isabel Wijsen were proud of the accomplishments Bye Bye Plastic Bags achieved and are quick to encourage youths. "Don't ever let anyone tell you that you're too young or you won't understand," says Isabel. "We're not telling you it's going to be easy. We're telling you it's going to be worth it."

Like Bali, the Gambia's plastic pollution contributes to carbon dioxide emissions and climate change. One woman in the Gambia, Isatou Ceesay, knows that when one abuses the environment, one abuses him or herself. For a long time, villagers dumped garbage behind their homes, resulting in disease and air pollution. In 1997, Ceesay and a team of women created the Recycling Centre of N'Jau. They educated others about the importance of waste management and recycling. They also taught women how to upcycle plastic bags into wallets, bags, and toys. These were sold, giving the women financial independence.

Ceesay worked with the Gambian government on a plastic bag ban. She says the following on Climateheroes.org:

> In order to love the environment, you must first love yourself. This is our responsibility to ensure that future generations do not ever live what we have been through. If we prepare children to become better leaders, and women to play an important part alongside men, then we will be able to mitigate climate change, while living and working in better conditions, and contributing to the development of our society. Everything is linked together.

Grassroot Connections with the Land

Activism organizations often start as grassroots causes. They are often built on an idea generated by one or several individuals. Dr. Vandana Shiva, born in India in 1952, was an integral part of grassroots campaigns to protect the diversity and integrity of living resources. She is a physicist and environmental activist and is especially interested in native seeds. Those types of seeds promote organic farming and fair trade.

In 1991, Shiva founded the grassroots organization Navdanya. It partners with farmers and communities to work against the homogenization of

Dr. Vandana Shiva, winner of the Sydney Peace Prize, plants seeds in a school garden while attending the 2010 Peace Festival in Australia.

crop production by large corporations like Monsanto. She opposes crops that are genetically modified organisms (GMOs) and the idea of corporations monopolizing the seed industry for profit. To fight this, Navdanya formed more than sixty seed banks in India and saved more than three thousand rice varieties. This has ensured sustainable methods of agriculture and significantly decreased the use of chemical fertilizers and pesticides. Dr. Shiva travels the world educating governments and organizations about sustainable practices.

In Harmony with the Environment

One of the world's most famous wildlife activists is Jane Goodall. She was born in England in 1934 and moved to Africa to live with and study more than one hundred Tanzanian chimpanzees. She ate with them, behaved like them, and learned the nuances of their caste system.

Chimpanzees have their own primitive language with well over twenty sounds. They have methods of comforting one another, rituals, and stones for weaponry. Goodall explains in books and lectures that we can learn from chimpanzees how they've lived for generations in harmony with their environment. Goodall partners with government officials, businesspeople, and tourism organizations to advocate for ecological responsibility. Her award-

Jane Goodall's activism helped her to receive a number of conservation awards and honors, including the National Geographic Society Centennial Award and being named a United Nations Messenger of Peace.

winning book *The Chimpanzee Family Book* teaches children how to respect wildlife in African nations populated by chimpanzees.

The Blue and Green Planet

Our oceans make up 97 percent of our planet's water. And while vast, they're vulnerable to global warming, overfishing, mining and drilling, ocean acidification, and pollution. American oceanographer and explorer Sylvia Earle encouraged the international community to band together in a 2009 TED talk when she said, "Our fate and the ocean's are one."

Earle is known for dozens of expeditions. She led the first all-female team to live underwater, walked untethered on the ocean floor, tracked marine mammals, and created undersea vehicle companies to help scientists reach new sea depths. In other words, Earle knows the world's oceans. To her, they're "the blue heart of the planet," because without them in full working order, we don't have a life support system. Earle calls for a global network of marine protected areas to cover 20 percent of the world's oceans by 2020. In her 2009 TED talk, she explains the importance of the ocean:

> With every drop of water you drink, every breath you take, you're connected to the sea. No matter where on Earth you live. Most of the oxygen in the atmosphere is generated by

BECOME A CHANGE MAKER: HOW TO GET STARTED IN ACTIVISM

Activism starts with an idea, grows with a plan, and relies on a team. If you're ready to be an activist, consider your community's most pressing needs. Perhaps there's already an organization that is working on that goal right now, one that would welcome your help. If not, consider starting your own grassroots team!

Next, decide if a one-time activity is sufficient or if an ongoing campaign is needed. Take stock of your resources. Do you have what you need now and for the long haul?

Then, evaluate who can help with the necessary funds and/or resources. How can each person add to the effort? For example, artists can make posters and design logos. Tech-savvy people can create and maintain websites and social media platforms. Those gifted with the powers of persuasion can write letters, meet with community leaders, and take care of outreach. If you need help, talk with a legal guardian, counselor, or mentor.

the sea. Over time, most of the planet's organic carbon has been absorbed and stored there, mostly by microbes. The ocean drives climate and weather, stabilizes temperature, shapes

Earth's chemistry. Water from the sea forms clouds that return to the land and the seas as rain, sleet and snow, and provides home for about 97 percent of life in the world, maybe in the universe. No water, no life; no blue, no green.

The greenery of the world also needs protecting and preservation. As a member in the National Council of Women of Kenya, Wangari Maathai (1940–2011) decided to plant trees to protect the environment. The idea caught on, and women's groups soon joined her. She founded the Green Belt Network, and together that organization planted more than fifty-one million trees around churches, farms, and schools.

The Green Belt Network's efforts led to the Pan African Green Belt Network in 1986, an organization that taught world leaders about conservation and environmental improvement. Tree-planting initiatives started in other countries such as Ethiopia, Tanzania, and Zimbabwe. Maathai also got involved in commissions, and she even served on the boards of the Jane Goodall Institute and Women's Environment and Development Organization. She received the Nobel Peace Prize in 2004.

CHAPTER SEVEN

EQUALITY ON THE JOB

I n the workplace, women have faced inequalities, discrimination, unequal pay, few benefits, and unhealthy work environments. Little by little, female activists have used their voices and taken actions to secure gains in the name of equality.

Working Hard for the Working Woman

With the Industrial Revolution in the eighteenth century came six-day workweeks of at least sixty hours, low pay, and no disability benefits. Workers breathed in harmful toxins and developed respiratory infections like pneumonia or tuberculosis. They also lost limbs and lives due to needless accidents. No safety measures were in place.

Mary Harris Jones leads striking textile workers on a march to draw attention to poor working conditions and unrealistic employer expectations.

The large population of workers needed representation. Labor unions popped up in Europe and the United States and advocated for education, new legislation, better working conditions, minimum wage, and benefits. For example, in 1866, newly freed black laundresses formed a union in Mississippi to strike for higher wages. In 1900, Lucy Parsons pulled together seven local unions to create the International Ladies' Garment Workers' Union. She later helped to organize the Industrial Workers of the World in 1905.

In 1903, schoolteacher Mary Harris Jones organized the Children's Crusade. It was a 125-mile (201-kilometer) march of child workers from mines and factories that demanded they go to school instead of work.

Ethnically diverse textile workers in Massachusetts initiated the 1912 Bread and Roses Strike. Marches, picketing, rally speeches, and clashes with armed authorities took place over nine weeks in the bitter winter. Women carried signs saying "We want bread, and roses, too." Their efforts led to a 15 percent increase in wages and overtime compensation.

Overall, union victories influenced improvements across the country and better legislation. In 1920, the Women's Bureau of the Department of Labor was created. It safeguarded working conditions for women and advanced their profit-making opportunities.

In 1925, Rosina Tucker organized the Brotherhood of Sleeping Car Porters, the first black labor union in the United States. Reverend Addie L. Wyatt (1924–2012) was another activist that advocated for women in the workplace. She got her start in 1941 with the Amalgamated Meat Cutters and Butcher Workmen of North America. She eventually became its president. She also learned from and participated in civil rights marches alongside Dr. Martin Luther King Jr.

In the 1960s, Eleanor Roosevelt appointed Wyatt to the Labor Legislation Committee of the Commission on the Status of Women. But what put Wyatt on the map was the Coalition of Labor Union Women (CLUW). She cofounded it in 1974, and it became the country's only national organization for union women. This group united more than twelve hundred union women from across the country. They became one voice for the millions of working women. CLUW organized their efforts for efficiency, promoted affirmative action, and encouraged female participation in policy-making efforts.

Workplace Harassment and Exclusion

Sexual harassment is subjecting victims to unwanted and sometimes repeated comments and/or advances of a sexual nature. It can cause stress, anxiety, and depression. If it happens at work, the work environment becomes a hostile one.

In 2013, the Uganda Human Rights Defenders Association (UHRDA) determined that 90 percent of women are sexually harassed at work by male supervisors. UHRDA studied 2,910 organizations, ranging from universities and churches to financial institutions and health-care centers. It found that a patriarchal system upholds the view that women are sex objects. It also found that victims fear they'll lose their jobs if they report the sexual harassment. They also fear that the perpetrator will go free.

The first female dean at the Makerere University's Law School in Uganda, law professor Sylvia Tamale, wanted to help victims speak up. She became a part of a yearlong, nationwide campaign to create awareness in businesses and in education institutions.

Members of the LGBTQ+ community also experience discrimination in the workplace. In many places, they fear that if they come out, they'll miss out on well-deserved raises, promotions, and professional development opportunities. Maki Muraki experienced this firsthand in Japan. While same-sex relationships are not illegal there, antidiscrimination laws do not protect LGBTQ+ individuals. What's more, there is a lack of education regarding LGBTQ+ rights.

Muraki has switched jobs five times because she never felt comfortable at work. The spaces were not queer friendly, and diversity programs only focused on female or disabled workers. While five times may not sound like much to some, leaving a job so many times is perceived as high turnover in a culture that promotes long-term employment.

Muraki conducted a 2013 survey in which she asked LGBTQ+ respondents about their experiences. They, too, faced difficulties that caused them to switch jobs. The environment they face contributed to anxiety and depression. It can also be costly for employers to have high turnover, as morale and productivity suffers from an unsteady workforce.

To help others like her, Muraki founded the nonprofit Nijiiro Diversity. It teaches about and promotes LGBTQ+ diversity and inclusion in the workplace. Nijiiro Diversity also consults corporations, such as Nissan, Panasonic, Sony, and

Tokyo Gas. Muraki stresses that an organization that is LGBTQ+ friendly is friendly to everyone.

Nurturing Democracy

Dolores Huerta was born in New Mexico in 1930. She was raised in the agricultural community of Stockton, California.

In 1962, she and Cesar E. Chavez started the National Farm Workers Association. It empowered migrant farmworkers, secured disability insurance, ensured the right to collectively organize, and bargained for increased wages and improved working conditions.

Huerta's efforts connected her to other influential activists. She met Gloria Steinem, and she began to fold ideals of challenging gender discrimination into her activism. Huerta knew that if she involved families in the farmworkers' movement—since adults and children all worked the fields—their efforts would be more effective. Huerta also traveled the United States for two years to encourage the Latina population to run for government offices.

Huerta won many awards, including the Eleanor Roosevelt Human Rights Award and was named one of the three most important women of 1997 by *Ms.* magazine. In 2012, Huerta received the Presidential Medal of Freedom. Her website, DoloresHuerta.org, shares her sentiments on the occasion:

Dolores Huerta (*left*) is pictured with Cesar Chavez. Together, they founded the National Farm Workers Association in 1962.

The freedom of association means that people can come together in organization to fight for solutions to the problems they confront in their communities. The great social justice changes in our country have happened when people came together, organized, and took direct action. It is this right that sustains and nurtures our democracy today. The civil rights movement, the labor movement, the women's movement, and the equality movement for our LGBT brothers and sisters are all manifestations of these rights.

Closing the Gender Pay Gap

Historically, females have not received equal pay for equal work. For every dollar earned by a male, a female earns only seventy-seven cents, according to unwomen.org. This twenty-three-cent difference is a global average, so it varies depending on where one works in the world.

In the 1800s, the United States gender pay gap caught national attention. Workers petitioned or went on strike for equal pay for equal work. For example, female New York City teachers fought the local board of education in 1911 to gain equal pay to their male colleagues. This worked, but it wasn't universal.

When men went to fight in World War I and II, females stepped into their jobs to help the war effort. The National War Labor Board decided female employees should receive equal pay. But after the wars, male veterans needed work, and the females were expected to tend to house and home.

Another victory for women in the United States came with the Equal Pay Act of 1963. It required employers to pay equal wages provided the same skill level, effort, and responsibility under similar working conditions existed within the same establishment. Legislation further protected females with the Civil Rights Act of 1964. It prohibited discrimination based on race, origin, color, religion, or gender. The Pregnancy Discrimination Act of 1978 prevents employers from treating females differently if they are pregnant, have given birth, or if they have related conditions. The Family and Medical Leave Act of 1993 requires employers to provide protected leave for qualifying family and medical purposes. The Lilly Ledbetter Fair Pay Act of 2009 was the next protection for equal pay.

THE LILLY LEDBETTER FAIR PAY ACT OF 2009

Lilly Ledbetter took on gender-based wage discrimination and brought about legislation that makes it possible for employees to file a lawsuit if subjected to lower pay than those of equal skill, effort, and responsibility.

(continued on the next page)

(continued from the previous page)

Ledbetter had worked for the Goodyear plant in Alabama for nearly twenty years and became one of the company's few female supervisors. Her boss told her that he didn't believe women should be in the workplace. To top it off, an anonymous note revealed the higher salaries of three male managers.

Ledbetter filed a complaint with the US Equal Employment Opportunity Commission and went to court. She was awarded back pay and about $3.3 million in compensatory and punitive damages. However, the Court of Appeals for the Eleventh Circuit reversed the verdict, saying that Ledbetter's case had

Lilly Ledbetter (*left of center, wearing a teal blazer*) looks on as President Barack Obama signs executive actions to enforce equal pay laws for women in 2014.

been filed too late. The Supreme Court upheld the decision, but Congress interceded. It determined that the time period for filing complaints was severely restricted. The House and Senate passed the Lilly Ledbetter Fair Pay Act of 2009, and President Obama signed it into law.

In the Spirit of Cooperation

It takes a committed group to affect change on any level. This means that women and their allies must work together. British public relations expert Lynne Franks understands this. Throughout her life, she has used her professional influence and contacts to influence change on a variety of activist issues. For example, she teamed up with Amnesty International to bring global awareness to human rights and to prevent the use of women as weapons of war in the Congo. She created Sustainable Enterprise and Empowerment Dynamics (SEED) to advocate for women's leadership across all walks of life, including war-torn regions, rural villages, prisons, and boardrooms. Franks encourages new leaders to rise up and get rid of the old ways of doing things. She favors fresh, innovative ideas that require collaboration. Franks told Helen Nianias of Independent.co.uk:

As women, we know that the best and most efficient way to get things done is to work together, and that means living and working with men in harmonious coexistence, valuing the perspectives and strengths of both sexes and creating a higher quality of life for all. It must also be a world of cooperation between business and community, human beings and the planet, national governments and nonprofit organizations, young and old, spirituality and science, and our inner and outer selves.

1777 Vermont abolishes slavery. Other Northern states follow suit in the coming decades.

1848 Lucretia Mott and Elizabeth Cady Stanton host the first women's rights convention in Seneca Falls, New York.

1865 Slavery is abolished in the United States through the ratification of the Thirteenth Amendment.

1881 Clara Barton starts the American Red Cross.

1893 New Zealand becomes the first country to grant women the right to vote.

1903 Marie Curie becomes the first female to receive the Nobel Peace Prize.

1908 Fifteen thousand women take to the streets in New York City calling for voting rights, shorter work hours, and better pay.

1911 The United States observes its third National Women's Day. Austria, Denmark, Germany, and Switzerland celebrate the first International Women's Day.

1916 Margaret Sanger opens the first US birth control clinic in New York City.

1920 The Nineteenth Amendment to the US Constitution grants women the right to vote; the Women's Bureau of the Department of Labor is established.

TIMELINE

1962 Dolores Huerta and Cesar E. Chavez start the National Farm Workers Association to give migrant farmworkers improved pay and working conditions.

1962 Eunice Kennedy Shriver hosts the first of many summer sports and physical activity camps. It is now known as the Special Olympics.

1964 The Civil Rights Act passes.

1974 Reverend Addie L. Wyatt founds the Coalition of Labor Union Women (CLUW).

1975 The UN celebrates International Women's Day (IWD) for the first time.

1993 The Family and Medical Leave Act passes.

2009 The Lilly Ledbetter Fair Pay Act is passed to give women equal pay for equal work.

2011 The International Day of the Girl Child is adopted by the United Nations General Assembly.

2015 Ireland passes the Gender Recognition Act.

2017 Five-year-old Sophie Cruz wins the Define American Award for Activist of the Year and addresses thousands at the Women's March on Washington.

GLOSSARY

autism spectrum disorder A range of developmental conditions affecting speech, nonverbal communication, and social skills.

caste system A social order in which status is inherited at birth. The system dictates where one can live, who one can marry, and what profession one can obtain.

cerebral palsy A condition caused by brain damage that causes little to no muscle control.

dioxins Chemical compounds that are poisonous to the body, causing any number of side effects such as altered liver function and immune system problems.

Down syndrome A disorder caused by a chromosome defect. It results in intellectual and physical challenges.

entrepreneur One who creates and builds one or more businesses.

ghee Butter fat that is commonly used in Indian cooking.

Islamist Describes radical conservative and intolerant views that claim to represent Islam and its adherents, Muslims.

midwife A medical professional whose job is to oversee childbirth.

misogyny The general mistrust, dislike, or hatred of those who identify as women.

mitigate The act of reducing or diminishing something, such as an effect, mistake, or symptom.

nonprofit organization (NPO) An organization that works toward some goal other than making money. Its services are primarily meant to improve a community.

obstetrics A branch of medicine that is concerned with childbirth.

patriarchal A society that is ruled by and controlled by men. It also benefits men more than any other group.

polio A virus transmitted via contact or contaminated food or water. It causes death or paralysis.

suffrage The right to vote and hold an elected office.

turnover The frequency of people or a person leaving a job over a set period of time. High turnover for a company indicates that the company cannot retain workers, and high turnover for an individual indicates that the individual doesn't stay in a job for long.

FOR MORE INFORMATION

American Association of University Women (AAUW)
1310 L Street NW, Suite 1000
Washington, DC 20005
(800) 326-2289
Website: http://www.aauw.org
Facebook: @AAUW.National
Instagram: @aauwnational
Twitter: @AAUW
YouTube: aauwinfo
AAUW uses advocacy, education, research, and
    philanthropy to gain gender equity for women
    and girls.

Association for Women's Rights in Development
    (AWID)
215 Spadina Avenue, Suite 150
Toronto, Ontario M5T 2C7
Canada
(416) 594-3773
Website: http://www.awid.org
Facebook and Instagram: @awidwomensrights
Twitter: @AWID
YouTube: @AWIDNews
AWID is dedicated to women's human rights, gender
    equality, and sustainable development.

Canadian Women's Foundation (CWF)
133 Richmond Street West, Suite 504
Toronto, ON M5H 2L3
Canada
(866) 293-4483
Website: http://www.canadianwomen.org
Facebook: @CanadianWomensFoundation
LinkedIn: @the-canadian-women's-foundation
Twitter: @cdnwomenfdn
YouTube: @CanadianWomenFdn
The CWF works to improve the lives of women
    and girls.

National Organization for Women (NOW)
    1100 H Street NW, Suite 300
    Washington, DC 20005
(202) 628-8669
Website: http://now.org
Facebook and Twitter: @NationalNOW
YouTube: @NOWvideos
NOW works to promote feminism, eliminate
    discrimination, and protect the rights of females.

Planned Parenthood Federation of America
123 William Street, 10th Floor
New York, NY 10038
(800) 430-4907
Website: http://plannedparenthood.org
Facebook: @PlannedParenthood
Instagram: @plannedparenthood
Twitter: @PPFA

YouTube: plannedparenthood
Planned Parenthood advocates for women's rights and
    health and wellness by offering reproductive health
    care, sex education, and family planning services.

United Nations Women (UN Women)
220 East 42nd Street
New York, NY 10017
Website: http://www.unwomen.org/en
Facebook, Instagram, and Snapchat:
    @unwomen
Twitter: @UN_Women
YouTube: @UNWomen
UN Women, an entity of the United Nations, advocates
    for gender equality and women's empowerment.

FOR FURTHER READING

Bonney, Grace. *In the Company of Women: Inspiration and Advice from Over 100 Makers, Artists, and Entrepreneurs*. New York, NY: Artisan, 2016.

Ebadi, Shirin. *Until We Are Free: My Fight for Human Rights in Iran*. New York, NY: Random House, 2016.

Ganda, Martin, and Caitlin Alifirenka. *I Will Always Write Back: How One Letter Changed Two Lives*. New York, NY: Little, Brown and Company, 2017.

Ignotofsky, Rachel. *Women in Science: 50 Fearless Pioneers Who Changed the World*. New York, NY: Ten Speed Press, 2016.

Schatz, Kate. *Rad Women Worldwide: Artists and Athletes, Pirates and Punks, and Other Revolutionaries Who Shaped History*. New York, NY: Ten Speed Press, 2016.

Shen, Ann. *Bad Girls Throughout History: 100 Remarkable Women Who Changed the World*. San Francisco, CA: Chronicle Books, 2016.

Stone, Tanya Lee. *Girl Rising: Changing the World One Girl at a Time*. New York, NY: Wendy Lamb Books, 2017.

Worden, Minky. *The Unfinished Revolution: Voices from the Global Fight for Women's Rights*. New York, NY: Seven Stories Press, 2012.

Yousafzai, Malala. *I Am Malala: How One Girl Stood Up for Education and Changed the World*. New York, NY: Little, Brown and Company, 2016.

BIBLIOGRAPHY

Daly, Clare. "Time 100: FGM Campaigner Jaha
    Dukureh Makes Prestigious List." *Guardian*, April
    21, 2016. https://www.theguardian.com
    /world/2016/apr/21/time-100-fgm-campaigner
    -jaha-dukureh-makes-prestigious-list.

Dolores Huerta Foundation. "Dolores Huerta."
    Retrieved August 26, 2017. http://doloreshuerta
    .org/dolores-huerta.

Dukureh, Jaha. "End Female Genital Mutilation in the
    US - Commission a Prevalence Report on Women
    Impacted and Girls at Risk." Change.org, 2013.
    https://www.change.org/p/end-fgm-now-protect
    -girls-from-getting-cut-and-support-victims-of-female
    -genital-mutilation-in-the-usa.

Franks, Lynne. *Grow: The Modern Woman's Handbook:
    How to Connect with Self, Lovers, and Others*.
    Carlsbad, CA: Hay House, 2004.

International Women's Day. "About International
    Women's Day (8 March)." Retrieved August 26,
    2017. https://www.internationalwomensday.com
    /About.

Jacobson, Casar. "Casar Jacobson."
    CasarJacobson.com. Retrieved August 26, 2017.
    http://casarjacobson.com.

Jeremyart on C-Span. "Ashton Kutcher Opening
    Statement." February 15, 2017. https://www.c
    -span.org/video/?c4656850/ashton-kutcher
    -opening-statement. Video.

Malala Fund. "Malala's Story." Retrieved September
    9, 2017. https://www.malala.org/malalas-story.

O'Doherty, Caroline. "Lydia Foy Recalls Hell of Being

Transgender During Childhood and School." *Irish Examiner*, November 3, 2014. http://www .irishexaminer.com/ireland/lydia-foy-recalls -hell-of-being-transgender-during-childhood-and -school-296017.html.

People. "Gloria Considers Gloria." January 27, 1992. http://people.com/archive/gloria-considers-gloria -vol-37-no-3.

Pisa, Katie. "Berta Cáceres' Family Seeks Justice on Anniversary of Fearless Activist's Death." CNN, March 3, 2017. http://www.cnn .com/2017/03/02/world/berta-caceres/index .html.

Riché, Max. "Satou Ceesay, Queen of Plastic Recycling in the Gambia." Climate Heroes. Retrieved August 19, 2017. http://climateheroes .org/portfolio-item/isatou-ceesay-queen-plastic -recycling-gambia.

Shakira. "Philanthropy." Retrieved August 26, 2017. http://www.shakira.com/philanthropy.

Special Olympics. "Special Olympics: Who We Are." Retrieved August 26, 2017. http://www .specialolympics.org/Sections/Who_We_Are /Who_We_Are.aspx.

TED. "Sylvia Earle." Retrieved August 17, 2017. https://www.ted.com/speakers/347.

United Nations. "International Day of the Girl Child 11 October." Retrieved August 26, 2017. http://www .un.org/en/events/girlchild.

UN Women. "Press Release: Activists, Celebrities and Governments Call to End Global Gender Pay Gap."

March 13, 2017. http://www.unwomen.org
/en/news/stories/2017/3/press-release
-activists-celebrities-and-governments-call-to-end
-global-gender-pay-gap.
Washington Post. "Lydia Cacho from Mexico."
September 12, 2015. https://www
.washingtonpost.com/video/national/most-good
-reporters–are-going-through-hell-to-be-responsible
-journalists-lydia-cacho-from-mexico/2015/09/11
/f5df6a00-57ef-11e5-9f54-1ea23f6e02f3_video
.html. Video.
Wijsen, Melati, and Isabel Wijsen. "Our Campaign to
Ban Plastic Bags in Bali." TED, September 2015.
https://www.ted.com/talks/melati_and_isabel
_wijsen_our_campaign_to_ban_plastic_bags_in
_bali.

INDEX

About the Author

After running a successful dance program for over a decade, Erin Staley took her stories from the stage to the page as a writer. Forever a student of the human condition, Staley fostered a passion for history, technology, and the enduring spirit of pioneers in their fields of interest. Today, she writes for the University of California, Riverside, as an international recruitment creative copywriter.

Photo Credits

Cover Dave J. Hogan/Getty Images; pp. 7, 86 Library of Congress, Prints and Photographs Division; p. 12 Everett Collection Historical/Alamy Stock Photo; pp. 14–15 Kevork Djansezian/Getty Images; p. 20 Official White House Photo by Pete Souza; pp. 22, 37, 40 © AP Images; p. 25 Library of Congress, Manuscript Division; pp. 28–29 John Olson/The LIFE Images Collection/Getty Images; pp. 32–33 Joerg Boethling /Alamy Stock Photo; p. 34 Shah Marai/AFP/Getty Images; p. 44 Everett Collection Inc./Alamy Stock Photo; p. 47 Haydn West /PA Images/Getty Images; p. 50 Museum of the City of New York/Archive Photos/Getty Images; p. 55 John Lamparski /Wirelmage/Getty Images; p. 57 Harry How/Getty Images; p. 60 Zacharias Abubeker/AFP/Getty Images; p. 63 Michael Gottschalk/Photothek/Getty Images; p. 67 Featureflash Photo Agency/Shutterstock.com; p. 71 EuropaNewswire/Gado /Archive Photos/Getty Images; p. 74 Orlando Sierra/AFP /Getty Images; p. 79 Craig Golding/Getty Images; p. 81 Bettmann/Getty Images; p. 91 Arthur Schatz/The LIFE Picture Collection/Getty Images; p. 94 Official White House Photo by Chuck Kennedy; cover and interior pages (gold) R-studio /Shutterstock.com.

Design and Layout: Nicole Russo-Duca; Photo Researcher: Nicole DiMella